If You Haven't Got a Prayer:

A Beginner's Guide to Talking with God

Stephen M. Crotts

InterVarsity Press
Downers Grove
Illinois 60515

InterVarsity Press is the book-publishing division of Inter-Varsity Christian Fellowship, a student movement active on campus at hundreds of universities, colleges and schools of nursing. For information about local and regional activities, write IVCF, 233 Langdon St., Madison, WI 53703.

Distributed in Canada through InterVarsity Press, 1875 Leslie St., Unit 10, Don Mills, Ontario M3B 2M5, Canada.

ISBN 0-87784-562-X

Printed in the United States of America

To my wife Kathryn,
herself an answer to prayer

1 IF YOU HAVEN'T GOT A PRAYER

In Ernest Hemingway's short story, *A Clean, Well-lighted Place,* an old waiter goes home after a long day's work in a café. On the way, he reflects on his life. He arrives at the conclusion that all his work comes to nothing. And he mumbles a prayer, but it is addressed to no one: Our Nothing who art in Nothing, Nothing be thy name. Thy Kingdom Nothing, thy will be Nothing in Nothing as it is in Nothing. Give us this Nothing our daily Nothing and Nothing us our Nothing as we Nothing our Nothings. And Nothing us not into Nothing but deliver us from Nothing.[1] Obviously the man didn't have a prayer. His prayers, like those of so many other people, turned to sawdust in his mouth or they bounced off the ceiling. They were nothing.

Many people, even Christians, admit that they haven't got a prayer. They say things like:

"I pray, but I seem to come up against a great cement wall. My prayers just don't seem to get beyond it."

"I just cannot pray anymore. It seems so useless."

"When I pray I just don't feel that God is listening."

"Why should I pray when I do not feel that God is at all interested in my personal problems?"

"I am frustrated with prayer. My mind wanders."

"Why doesn't God answer me?"

How about you? Are you like Hemingway's character? Do you attempt to pray but feel it is all nothing? Perhaps, unlike him, you firmly believe that God exists, but in practice—in your prayer life— the effect is the same. You are a practical atheist; there is no communication.

You are not alone. Many do not have a prayer. Nor did the original disciples at one time. And they were concerned about it.

In Luke 11 we are told that the disciples watched while Jesus was praying. The Lord seemed to talk with God so naturally. His words came out simply, sincerely. Why, it was almost as if Christ were a son having a discussion with a caring father. "How does he do it?" they wondered. "What is his secret?" They were impressed. And they wanted tutoring. "Lord, teach us to pray," they pleaded (11:1).

Are you willing to ask the Lord to teach you to pray? Are you willing to join with Christ in the school of prayer? If you are, then you can learn to talk with God. You can learn to overcome the obstacles that have kept you from prayer.

My Mind Wanders One of the first obstacles to prayer is a wandering mind. We all know how this is. We sit down in the chair, earnestly begin to pray and end up thinking about our bills or wondering if we answered question 5 correctly on the psychology quiz we just took.

A wandering mind has hindered the prayer life of many. John Wesley was once preaching in England about how few people had an adequate prayer life. After his sermon was over, a man came up to him and began to brag about his prayer life. "The Lord and I are close," he said. "We can talk about anything."

Wesley looked at him and said, "Is that so? I bet you my horse you cannot even pray for thirty minutes without your mind wandering." The bet was made. Right there in public the man knelt down and began to pray aloud. He did well. For five minutes he prayed for forgiveness. For another ten minutes he prayed for all the missionaries around the world. Then he began to pray for more understanding. He was well into his prayers when he suddenly opened his eyes and said, "By the way, Mr. Wesley, do I get the saddle along with the horse as well?"

Everyone who has ever tried to pray has, like this man, had problems with drifting thoughts. Prayer is like turning your radio on. With the music comes static. You can tune a lot of the interference out but occasionally a crackle still gets through.

We too can tune much of the static out of our prayer lives. Try keeping a prayer list in a small notebook. In it write down everything that you want to pray about. Then throughout the day and especially during your prayer time go through the list and make your requests known before the Lord.

You might also try praying aloud. Voicing your prayers rather than just thinking them helps keep your mind from wandering and makes your prayers more definite and active. Between the list and praying aloud you should be able to stay on the wavelength and out of the static. But do not expect too much. People experienced in prayer will tell you that a wandering mind is a constant frustration. Work at it. You will improve.

I Fall Asleep Here is another common complaint: "I get into bed to say my prayers at night and before I know it I fall asleep." Well, what a wonderful way to go to sleep! And how pleasing to our heavenly Father it must be to have us crawl up into his lap to talk with him and fall asleep there!

Bedtime prayers are a good way to spend our last waking moments. But if that is the only time we make for prayer it is not adequate. C. S. Lewis said,

> *No one in his senses . . . would reserve his chief prayers for bed-time–obviously the worst possible hour for any action which needs concentration. . . . My own plan, when hard-pressed, is to seize any time, and place, however unsuitable, in preference to the last waking moment. On a day of traveling . . . I'd rather pray sitting in a crowded train than put it off till midnight. . . . On other, and slightly less crowded, days a bench in a park, or a back street where one can pace up and down, will do.*[2]

Lewis's remarks are valid. Bedtime prayers are good but inadequate. Why not set aside a time each day when you are alert and pray at that time? If you are a student, pray during your afternoon break. If you are a housewife, pray when the children are napping. If you are a commuter, pray on the way to work in traffic.

I Don't Have Any Time! "I don't have time!" people say. "In the morning I am up and off like a shot. My feet don't touch the ground till supper." I have a friend for whom the pace of life is an obstacle to prayer. He has to drive fifteen miles to work each day. The traffic is always heavy. It used to be that by the time this man reached his desk he was so tense no one dared to cross him. It took until three o'clock for his nerves to relax and his temper to cool. But by then it was almost time for him to go home. After another hour of traffic, he was irritable again, snapping at his children and cross with his wife.

I asked him what he did during those long hours in the car going to and from work. "I fuss at the man who pulled in front of me, and fume over all the time I waste!" he replied. After we had studied some Scripture on prayer together, I challenged him. "You're a Christian, sir. Why don't you use the time going to work to pray for yourself and your family? Then use the time coming home to pray for others."

A year passed before I visited again. But when I saw him, his face told the story. "It really works!" he said. "Not only am I now praying as I should, but I'm so much easier to live with. I get to the office relaxed and arrive home the same."

You too probably find time for prayer scarce. But if you

will take a creative look at your day, you will certainly find a place to fit in thirty minutes or so of conversation with the Lord. You can pray on the way to work, while you walk the dog, cultivate the garden, hang out the clothes, or just relax in a chair.

Why Doesn't God Answer Me? Another problem people often have with prayer is summed up in the complaint, "Why doesn't God answer me? I've prayed and I've prayed for something and the Lord just hasn't heard me." In Isaiah 65:24 God says, "Before they call I will answer, while they are yet speaking I will hear." You can believe that the Lord hears every prayer you make. And you can be sure that he always answers you. But here is the catch. There are many answers to prayer. God may say Yes, No, Wait awhile, or he may guide you to an option or open a door you had not even imagined. What would you think of a six-year-old boy who, when father wisely says No to his request for a shotgun, slumps into a chair and says, "Dad didn't hear me. He won't answer me." Many of our complaints about prayer are like that. "Why doesn't God answer me?" we query. What we really mean to say is, "Why doesn't the Lord see things my way and give me what I want?"

As Christians we must realize that we are children praying to a loving heavenly Father. He has our best interests at heart. He would never overindulge us, give us something that would harm us, or insulate us from an experience we need to go through to develop character.

Though we can be confident he hears all our prayers, we must understand that No is as valid an answer as Yes or Wait awhile. Christ recognized this aspect of prayer. In the Garden of Gethsemane he prayed, in effect, "Lord, let this cup pass from me. I don't want to be crucified. Find some other way!" He was praying that God would see it his way. "Let your answer be Yes," he was pleading. But then Jesus showed he was willing for the answer to be otherwise. He said, "Nevertheless not my will, but thine, be done" (Lk. 22:42). And he went to the cross to die for our sins.

We too should pray following Christ's example. Go ahead and talk to the Lord. Tell him just how you feel. He hears you. But trust him, trust his answer. Submit to his right to be the Father and to exercise his judgment over his children. Allow him to say Yes or No or Wait awhile. (The question of unanswered prayer will be discussed further in a later chapter.)

How Do I Say It? Another roadblock to prayer is confusion over physical posture and over what words to use. "I just don't know what to say. I mean it's not just anybody that I am talking to. That's God Almighty himself! What do I say? What words do I use? I just don't know how to pray."

I suppose the church has frightened people away from prayer simply by perpetuating the idea that God must be addressed in lofty, King James language. Have you ever heard an elder pray like this: "Holy Father and infinite Jehovah, we beseech thee, look down upon us, thy humble servants, and in thine infinite mercy and with thy ineffable love grant the petitions of our hearts"? Such prayers discourage us from praying. What is communicated is that unless you talk like this you cannot pray to God.

But did you know that the Bible does not tell us how we should pray—eyes open or closed, sitting, kneeling, standing or lying; for a few seconds, for thirty minutes or all night; with lofty language or simple words? Scripture tells us of men and women who spoke to God in all kinds of postures. Moses lifted his arms to pray. Others folded their hands. Some prostrated themselves face down. Jesus knelt.

The Bible also tells us of men and women who spoke to God in all kinds of situations. Daniel prayed from the lion's den. Solomon prayed from his palace. Paul prayed in prison. Joshua prayed in military victory. Christ talked to God in a garden.

Bible characters spoke to God out of various attitudes and emotions. Moses prayed with fervor and respect. David prayed while sinful and depressed. Paul prayed with confidence. Others prayed with joy. Christ prayed with pain while dying on the cross.

This little poem by Sam Walter Foss humorously expresses the point:

"The proper way for a man to pray,"
Said Deacon Lemuel Keyes,
"And the only proper attitude
Is down upon his knees."
"Nay, I should say the way to pray,"

Said the Reverend Doctor Wise,
"Is standing straight with outstretched arms
And rapt and upturned eyes."
"Oh, no, no, no," said Elder Snow,
"Such posture is too proud.
A man should pray with eyes fast closed
And head contritely bowed."
"It seems to me his hands should be
Austerely clasped in front.
With both thumbs pointing toward the ground,"
Said Reverend Doctor Blunt.
"Las' year I fell in Hodgkin's well
Head first," said Cyrus Brown,
"With both my heels a-stickin' up,
My head a-pointing down;
An' I made a prayer right then an' there–
Best prayer I ever said,
The prayingest prayer I ever prayed,
A-standing on my head!"[3]

You can pray just as well standing on your head in a well as you can on your knees in a chapel. You can pray to God any time, any place and with any words just as long as you are sincere.

Some may still have difficulty breaking through the "verbal barrier," the point when you want to pray, feel the need to pray, but just don't know what to say. How do I get the words to come? How *do* I talk to God? For starters, let's not think of prayer as work, as having to come up with new thoughts to express to God. Begin with what is already on your mind, with what preoccupies you. Simply express these things *to God.* People ordinarily spend a good deal of "computer time" ruminating over and worrying about many things. Address these inner musings, dialogs, conflicts, bitterness, happiness or appreciation (of landscape, a child, music, or whatever) *to God.* This may be a very practical and meaningful way for you to break through into prayer. Prayer need not be a stuffy, artificial exercise like writing a term paper.

Others have found using Scripture in prayer not only provides the words that come so hard, but a depth of meaning as well that otherwise might not be possible at 6 A.M. or during a 15-minute break in the day. The psalms, being prayers, are excellent for this. Take one and pray it to God. Let it suggest the direction of your prayer. Stop and elaborate on a verse or two of praise or confession. You'll be surprised how close the psalms will be to your own sentiments and they will school you in prayer as well. (See "Make a Bible Your Prayer Book," *HIS,* Jan. 1974, p. 26.)

The fellowship of other Christians may be of further help in learning to pray. I find it a very helpful practice to read prayers that others have written down. Just seeing what they said and how they said it quite often enables me to pray more effectively. It is like looking over a craftsman's shoulder to see how he works. You might want to ask your minister to write down some prayers for you or perhaps you could purchase a book of prayers to read.

A Declaration of Dependence So far we have looked at

barriers to prayer like wandering minds, drowsiness, not knowing how to pray and unanswered prayer. But perhaps the greatest hindrance to prayer is the feeling that it is unnecessary.

In 1776 the thirteen American colonies declared their independence from England. They told King George that they did not want him or need him anymore. And so it was that the colonists formed their own government and struck out on their own. The third chapter of Genesis teaches that the human race once rebelled against God and declared its independence from him. This rebellion is still very much with us. Most of us feel that we can take care of ourselves. We see no need to praise God or confess our sins or give thanks. When we need something we just buy it.

How does God respond to our independent spirit? He pushes us. He shoves us beyond independence to dependence. Often as a pastor I have counseled people in times of crisis. I hear them say, "I've tried everything. And now all my money, all my education and connections have been to no avail. Pastor, can God help me? I'm at the end of my rope."

Prayer is a recognition that God exists. It is agreeing that God has authority over us. It is a confession to God, "I need you as a child needs his father." And such a declaration of dependence comes hard to our rebel hearts. All too often it comes only as a last resort.

What about you? Have you made your declaration of dependence to God or are you still too proud to pray? Your

Christian life should not be a kind of panic religion which is used only when you are at the end of your rope. So if you have not done so, make sure right now that God knows you depend on him. This recognition will remove the last obstacle to a lifestyle of living dialog with God.

You've Got God's Undivided Attention! Remember the nursery rhyme about the little old lady who lived in a shoe? She had so many children she didn't know what to do. Some people think God is like that; he has so many children he cannot possibly listen to them all. But nothing could be further from the truth. Such thinking makes the Lord smaller than he is. The Bible says that God knows your very name (Is. 43:1) and that even the hairs of your head are numbered (Mt. 10:30). We can cast all our anxieties on God because he cares for us (1 Pet. 5:7).

Together these promises and assurances are an impressive encouragement to prayer. You've got a prayer! Why not use it? Why not ask God right now to help you deal with the obstacles that have hindered your way to him in prayer? Why not say with the disciples, "Lord, teach me to pray"?

We once tried an experiment in church. I asked each person to think of a favorite hymn. Then on signal everyone stood up and began to sing their favorite hymns at the same time. After some moments of loud, chaotic singing, the congregation grew quiet. You may think that was rather impolite to the Lord. Not really. Every Sunday morning the same kind of thing goes on. The Methodists are singing their hymns while the Episcopalians down the street are singing theirs; Presbyterians are making their melodies and thousands of other Christian churches around the world are doing the same. To us it seems confusing. But to God it is beautiful indeed.

It is the same when God listens to his children pray. Thousands are praying at once, but each has God's full attention. Just as he hears every song, so he hears every prayer from his people. He is a loving Father and takes pleasure in conversing with his children.

2 TALK TO HIM

The French writer Voltaire published the lively story of *Candide* in 1759. In it, Candide, a world traveler, arrives in South America and discovers the utopian civilization at El Dorado. As he is preparing to meet the King, Candide asks about the customs of that area. He wants to know what is the proper way to greet his Majesty. He asks if he should kneel or stand. Should his hands be on his head or at his back? He wonders if he should lick the dust of the throne room floor or if some other gesture is expected.

Amused, an officer replies that the custom in his country for greeting the King is to simply embrace him.[4]

The Bible likewise teaches prayer devoid of any pompous ceremony. We simply approach God in faith and embrace him as a child does his papa. Jesus instructed his disciples to pray directly to the Father: "When you pray, say: Our Father. . . ." (Lk. 11:2). The apostle Paul stressed this truth as well. While encouraging the Christians at

Rome about their relationship to God, he says, "You have received the spirit of sonship. When we cry, 'Abba! Father!' it is the Spirit himself bearing witness with our spirit that we are children of God" (Rom. 8:15-16). Paul uses the Aramaic word *abba* which is best translated "dad" or "daddy." We can be as familiar with God as a son is with his father. When we pray, we can say, "Dad, . . ." for "[in Christ] we have boldness and confidence of access [to God] through our faith in him" (Eph. 3:12).

Since we have direct contact with God and his full attention, what should we say when we talk to him? How should we pray? How do we embrace him?

Praise the Lord! In the Lord's Prayer, Jesus taught his disciples first to praise God. "Pray then like this: Our Father who art in heaven, *hallowed be Thy name*" (Mt. 6:9). This is simply an ascription of worth. It is saying, "God, our Father, you are in heaven, you are over all and you are holy and worthy of praise!"

The dictionary defines praise as, "A confirmation and due acknowledgement of the great and wonderful excellences and perfections that are in God." And did you know that much of your Bible is praise? The prophets praise God for his justice. Job praises God while hurting. The psalmist, while viewing nature, cries out, "O LORD, our Lord, how majestic is thy name in all the earth!" (Ps. 8:1). The angels praise God (Lk. 2:13; Rev. 7:11-12). Paul even praised the Lord from prison (Acts 16:25).

If we were honest, I am quite certain most of us would

have to admit that our prayers seldom include much praise. Too often we only pray when we need something. We treat God like some sort of divine bellhop. "Do this. Do that. Carry this. Take that away. Bring me this!" But we should not pray to God only because we want him to do something. He is God! He is the Creator and Sustainer of the universe. That alone makes him worthy of our praise.

After a week of revival services in a small town, a little lady named Hallie was seen walking down the street carrying a bucket of water and a crowbar. Most people in town thought Hallie was a bit crazy anyway, and a lot of folks called out to her, "Hey, Hallie! Where are you going with that bucket of water and that crowbar?" Hallie answered, "I'm going to tear up heaven with this crowbar, and put out the fires of hell with this water. Then people will have to praise God because he is God and not because of what he can do for them!" Maybe Hallie has more sense than she is given credit for. God is God and, quite apart from what he can do to us or for us, he is worthy of our praise.

Do you remember Jacob in the Bible? He married Leah. And together they had a son called Judah. Now *Judah* is a Hebrew name which means "praise." In other words, they named their son Praise. Judah became the head of one of the twelve tribes of Israel. Later, during the Exodus, Moses constructed the tent of worship in the wilderness and God instructed each of the twelve tribes of Israel to camp around the tent. There was only one doorway into that tent of meeting and God commanded that Judah's tribe camp in front of the entrance. In other words, praise stands at the entrance into the Lord's presence.

This is what Psalm 100 teaches as well. It says, "Enter ... his courts with praise!" (v. 4). This is why we first praise God as a congregation when we worship together. It is our entrance into God's presence.

In your own private prayers, you may want to begin with praise. It could take the form of a hymn where you sing, "O For a Thousand Tongues to Sing My Great Redeemer's Praise." It could take the form of a psalm where you acclaim, "Bless the LORD, O my soul; and all that is within me, bless his holy name!" (Ps. 103:1). Or just praise God in your own words. And you can praise God in all circumstances, not just when things are going your way. When you are depressed there is no better tonic for your spirit than praising the Lord. The same is true of defeat, fear, frustration, hardship, pain and confusion. Praise lifts your spirit right up to God's throne. It carries you into God's presence.

Lord, Have Mercy on Me, a Sinner A second way Jesus taught us to pray is found also in the Lord's Prayer. "Father ... forgive us our sins" (Lk. 11:4). Here Jesus is showing us that at least part of our prayer time should be spent confessing our sins. Jesus illustrated this attitude in prayer with a story.

> *"Two men went up into the temple to pray, one a Pharisee and the other a tax collector. The Pharisee stood and prayed thus with himself, 'God, I thank thee that I am*

not like other men, extortioners, unjust, adulterers, or even like this tax collector. I fast twice a week, I give tithes of all that I get.' But the tax collector, standing far off, would not even lift up his eyes to heaven, but beat his breast, saying, 'God, be merciful to me a sinner!' " [Then Jesus said,] *"I tell you, this man went down to his house justified rather than the other." (Lk. 18:10-14)*

Right here in black and white from the pages of Scripture is the Lord's insistence that we see ourselves not as we think we are, or as others say we are, but as God says we are—sinful. Paul said, "All [Christians included] have sinned and fall short of the glory of God" (Rom. 3:23). "Surely there is not a righteous man on earth who does good and never sins" (Eccles. 7:20). God insists that we recognize our sins and confess them to him.

As you live your life in Christ, you are certain to find the Spirit bringing to your consciousness specific sins. Jesus said of the Spirit, "He will convince the world concerning sin" (Jn. 16:8). He will not overwhelm you by revealing too many of your sins at one time. That would crush you. He will do it little by little so you can handle it. He may convict you of a mind full of lust. He may point out a gossiping tongue, a critical spirit or an unjust business habit. And when he does convict you of that sin, God expects you to repent. He expects you to confess that sin asking for forgiveness and release from its bondage.

Confession is great therapy. It is a form of prayer that strips away our guilt and clears our consciences; that acknowledges our brokenness and takes us to the Divine Healer; that breaks the sin habit and builds character. It is healing therapy for broken people. It brings life. It was David's prayer of confession (see Ps. 32 and 51) that restored him after an adulterous affair with Bathsheba. It was the prayer of the thief on the cross that prompted Jesus' promise of paradise. It was Isaiah's prayer of confession in Isaiah 6 that was followed by his commissioning as a prophet. And it is our prayers of confession as well that bring us nearer to God, that make us more Christlike, and that equip us to serve the Lord.

During World War I, fighter pilots used to fly airplanes constructed out of wire, cloth and wood. Occasionally while flying, a pilot would hear a gnawing sound coming from the back of the plane. It was a dreaded sound. A rat had crawled into his grounded aircraft and was now eating away at the cloth and the wood. If he chewed through a cable, the pilot would lose control of his plane and crash. So he would quickly execute a procedure known as "taking the rat up." The pilot would simply climb for all the altitude he could get and, since rats cannot breathe thin air, the rat would die and the plane would be saved. Our confessional prayers work something like that. When we find a "rat" in our lives, some sin that threatens to hurt us or destroy us, we should take it up to God in prayer. Sin cannot exist in God's presence. His holiness destroys it.

If the Holy Spirit is convicting you of a sin, go to God in prayer. Bare your feelings to him. Be completely honest. Open your life up before his eyes. Pray with the Psalmist,

"Search me, O God, and know my heart! Try me and know my thoughts! And see if there be any wicked way in me" (Ps. 139:23-24). Then expose the sin directly before God. Admit that you have done it. Blush over it in God's presence. If you pray like that, you will either stop the sin or you will stop the prayer!

Thank the Lord! Jesus taught yet another form of prayer. Do you recall how Christ healed ten men of leprosy? Yet only one returned to give thanks to God. Sorely disappointed, Jesus said, "Were not ten cleansed? Where are the nine?" (Lk. 17:17). At least part of our conversation with God should be thanksgiving. We should be like the one leper who, finding himself clean, returned to say, "Thank you."

It is thanksgiving prayer that reminds us of our blessing and acknowledges God as our source of blessing. It is thanks prayer that keeps us from sins of grumbling, complaining and cynicism. It is thanks prayer that builds gratitude, pleasantness and loyalty into our character. It is thanks prayer that turns our whining into whistling.

Have you ever heard these complaints? A store clerk says, "I have to work so hard. No one's job is as hard as mine!" A man in the living room of his fine home grumbles, "This profession isn't what it used to be. You can't make any money anymore!" When it rains people say, "What a messy day." When the sun shines they say, "It's too hot."

I know a family that practices thanksgiving to the exclusion of whining. They observe Thanksgiving not just once a year like most people, but any time they have something for which they are greatly thankful. They plan a feast, invite others over and have a regular Thanksgiving supper. In the past year, they have had seven Thanksgivings for such things as a college graduation, a new grandchild, a successful operation and a new puppy. You may want to follow their example.

From time to time reflect on your life and walk with God; consider how God has worked through people, events and his Spirit to shape you. If you keep a prayer list, go back frequently and examine it to see where the yes-answered prayers are. Next pray, "Lord, you have given me so much. Give one thing more, a grateful heart." Then very simply thank the Lord for sharing his strength with you when you wanted to quit. Thank him for helping you to show someone close to you that you care. Thank him for giving you the words to say when your son had turned his back. Thank the Lord for allowing you to talk with him as a friend. Thank him for bringing you the courage to mention Jesus to a friend. Thank him for comforting you when someone you loved died.

Prayer may be compared to driving a car with a manual transmission. Just as there are different gears in a car, so there are different gears in prayer. No one drives a car with manual transmission without shifting gears. That would be an abuse. Different road conditions and speeds demand different gears. Prayer is like that too. It is an abuse of prayer to pray one way all of the time. It is abuse to pray only when you need something.

We start off our prayers with praise—first gear. We shift into confessional prayer—second gear. Now we are really beginning to get going. So we shift again into thanks prayer—third gear. Like Jesus said, we are really talking to "Our Father."

Why not experiment with these three forms of prayer right now? First, praise the Lord. Say or sing it aloud. Don't be afraid of your voice. Next, pray confessionally. Ask the Holy Spirit to point out sin in your life. "Take the rat up" to God. Ask his forgiveness. Finally, thank the Lord. Right now, say what you are thankful for. "Lord, you have given so much! Give one thing more, a grateful heart!"

Talk to Him of Needs When I went off to college, my father gave me a blank check with his signature on it. I would be several hundred miles away from home, living in a strange city and did not know what my expenses would be; so Dad trusted me with such a check. With it I could meet any situation with financial confidence. And, believe me, it was a comfort to know that the name of my father along with all his resources stood behind me.

Prayer is like that blank check. We are God's children making our way through this world. We are far from home, we do not know what our expenses will be, but we have confidence in the fact that our heavenly Father stands behind us with his full resources.

Christ was eager for his disciples to grasp that God was giving them a blank check to carry with them through life.

"Whatever you ask in my name, I will do it, that the Father may be glorified in the Son; if you ask anything in my name, I will do it" (Jn. 14:13-14). In other words, Jesus was doing for his disciples what my father did for me when I left for college: he was giving them his name along with his complete backing. And to make certain his disciples heard what he was saying, he repeated this promise four times in John 14—16.

This access to God's resources never ceased to amaze the early disciples. "We have Christ's name!" the apostles confidently affirmed. And in the Gospel of John, we find numerous meditations on the name of Christ and his marvelous resources. Jesus is called "the Christ," "Son of God," "King," "Son of man," "bread of life," "light of the world," "good shepherd," "the way, the truth and the life." With such a name for authority, is there any wonder Christians still end their prayers by saying, "In Christ's name I ask it, Amen"? The apostle Paul, traveling far from home, knew of and believed in God's blank check policy of prayer. He assured other Christians of the Lord's full backing when he said, "My God will supply every need of yours according to his riches in glory in Christ Jesus" (Phil. 4:19). He was saying, "You write the check. God will back you for all your needs."

Intercessory Prayer It is these promises of God in particular that give us confidence for prayers of intercession. Jesus taught us to pray for one another by setting an example. In John 17 Christ prayed for his disciples and for all who would believe in him. In Luke 22:31-32 Jesus revealed that he had been praying for Peter. And throughout the Gospels we find the Lord praying for the blind, the lame, the sinful and the mute.

Likewise, we who follow Jesus Christ should pray for one another. But the tragedy is that we seldom do. We piously say, "I will pray for you." But our intentions seldom become a reality. When someone is ill, facing huge decisions, or grappling with some problem, we often go to great extremes to help them. We call to encourage them. We send them a card. We take over a casserole. We might even loan them some money or send flowers. This is all good, but it stops short of our best service—prayer.

Hallmark Greeting Card Company advertises its product with the slogan, "When you care enough to send the very best." That is what we are talking about here. Perhaps the best others can do is visit and bring a gift, but Christians can pray. We have God's name and resources behind us to help our friends. James 5:16 says, "Pray for one another." Do the very best you can for your neighbors.

Let's suppose that you look out your window and happen to see your friend's child high up in a tree. He seems about to fall. What do you do? (a) Ignore the whole situation. You cannot climb trees so you cannot help. (b) Carry his mother some flowers and make a donation to a favorite charity. (c) Write a note of sympathy and offer your condolences. Both b and c? No, the best thing you can do when you witness something like that is to quickly call the child's parents and tell them the situation. That one act will do more good than anything else. Mom will go out to assure the frightened child that everything is going to be all right. Dad will call the fire department and they will rush over with their safety net and big ladder.

Intercessory prayer works like this, too. It informs God of your concern. It brings the comfort of the Holy Spirit. Like the phone call, it sets in motion the forces that bring relief.

The next time you see someone in need, tell God about it. He may want to use you to meet that need. Or he may have other plans. But whatever the situation, draw on your full resources. Go straight to the top. First tell God, then do what you can yourself.

Throughout the Bible, we find examples of the people of God praying about war and famine, for the ordinary functioning of government and for justice in human affairs (2 Chron. 32:20; Jas. 5:17-18; 1 Tim. 2:1-2; Hab. 1:1-4). While certainly our family, friends and ourselves are to be an important part of our prayers, we should not therefore neglect the "big" problems in our intercession. Storms, wars, political upheavals or oppression all greatly affect the lives of thousands of people. These things matter to our sovereign God and they should matter to us as well, for they are implied in Jesus' instruction to his disciples to pray "Thy kingdom come, Thy will be done, on earth as it is in heaven" (Mt. 6:10).

May I Pray For Myself? That we should pray for others

is seldom questioned. But some still wonder, "Is it O.K. to pray for myself?" Jesus prayed for himself in the Garden of Gethsemane (Lk. 22:41-42). There he prayed, "Father, if thou art willing, remove this cup from me." Also, Paul by his example teaches us to pray for ourselves. In 2 Corinthians 12:8 Paul confesses that he prayed for his own personal healing three times.

A nurse, accustomed to working with her hands, developed a prayer routine using her fingers as a guide. Her thumb, being nearest to her body, reminded her to pray for those close to her—family and friends. The index or pointer finger was a symbol of those who direct and manage. It reminded her to pray for her supervisors. The middle finger, tallest of all, stood for those in high positions of leadership and government. Her ring finger, the weakest, reminded her to pray for those who suffer. Finally, the little finger, last and smallest of all, she took to represent herself. Thus with meekness she expressed her own needs last. That's not a bad plan for petition prayers. Putting yourself last, but not least, is a good formula.

Since praying for myself is just as correct as praying for others, another question arises. "Can I pray to God about anything, or is the Lord just interested in big things?" The rule here is very simple. "Cast all your anxieties on him, for he cares about you" (1 Pet. 5:7). In other words, if something is big enough to cause you anxiety, it is big enough to pray about. Remember, the hairs of your head are numbered, and not even a sparrow falls from the sky without God's knowledge. Your concerns are God's concerns. Is your budget worrying you? Tell God. Is your child rebellious? Take it to the Lord in prayer. Toothaches, injustices, exams, marriages, backaches, hurt feelings and money worries—this is the stuff of life. And God has given us a blank check. We have the name of Christ behind us; his full resources are at our disposal. Tell God. Draw on his resources. He cares.

In the small town of Atotonilco, Mexico, there is a Catholic church. In that church there is a chapel with a statue of Christ dressed in a purple robe. The townspeople frequently go before this statue to pray for their problems. When I visited that church years ago, I too knelt there to pray. It was then that I noticed what the people had been doing. There at the feet of Christ were little folded pieces of paper. I unfolded several and read things like, "Lord, heal my baby." "Jesus, help my crop to grow." Another said, very simply, "My wife, Rosita." As I rose to leave I also noticed that people were not only leaving their petitions at the feet of Jesus, they were also pinning them on his robe. Little trinkets like those from a charm bracelet were hanging from Christ's robe. Some were in the shape of a baby, a house, or a leg. That is a literal, physical illustration of what 1 Peter 5:7 tells us to do in our prayers: "Cast all your anxieties on him, for he cares about you."

3 WHEN YOU'VE MASTERED THE BASICS

Now that you know more about how to pray and what to pray for, you are ready to move on to some of the deeper levels of a personal prayer life. These include praying with others and learning to listen to God.

Praying with Others Once you have become acquainted with the methods of individual prayer, you should learn more about group prayer. Too often, we feel as though our spiritual lives are simply a matter between us and God. We think that the Christian life is just another form of individualism.

This is not true. When Christ established his church, he had in mind a fellowship of believers. He did not want simply the worship of people as individuals; he wanted the church as a whole to worship him as one body. Therefore, if we are truly to know the power of prayer, we must discover group prayer.

In group prayer, we share our deepest needs with each other and God at the same time. We also recognize our dependence on other believers for love and support. Christ wants us to depend on each other. It is only as we do so that we can fully know the meaning of the kingdom of God. John Paterson in the booklet *How to Pray Together* lists the following reasons why we should regularly participate in group prayer:

(1) Prayer in groups enables individuals to pray with more assurance. When praying alone, you usually ask for things you want. So perhaps you cautiously qualify your prayers–"If it is Your will"–to cover your uncertainty. When other people share the same prayer concern, you can pray more confidently, knowing that you are not just pursuing personal whims. Recall Christ's promise that "if two of you agree on earth about anything they ask, it will be done for them by my Father in heaven" (Mt. 18:19).

(2) Prayer in groups builds Christian fellowship. In fact, prayer unites groups more quickly than almost any other activity. Sharing in prayer draws you into a closer bond and understanding of the others in the prayer group. As you listen to other people pray, you learn what God has taught them.

(3) Prayer in groups expresses a spiritual truth. The Christian life is a life with others. The Bible describes the Christian life as membership in a body–family life in a household. The work that God has for His family to do is such that the prayer meeting becomes the family

business meeting–and the business requires your attention.[5]

Group prayer is another means of gaining maturity. Jesus not only taught us to pray in secret behind closed doors (Matthew 6:5-8), he also taught us to pray in the presence of other believers. The early church, according to Acts 1:14 and 12:5, met frequently for group prayer. It is clear, then, that our prayer life is not merely an individual habit. It is a public practice as well.

In a prayer group you will be nurtured by others, and will, in time, be able to support them as you yourself mature. Go ahead and seek out a number of other believers. Arrange for a time and place to meet for an hour. And when you come together, take time to share your burdens, joys, doubts and needs. Then as a group make your needs known to God. You might try singing your praise and gratitude. You can try praying silently or out loud one at a time. The Holy Spirit will lead you to the best method for your group.

God Listens, You Listen Too Prayer is a dialog, not a monolog. It is a conversation between two people—God and the Christian. We must listen as well as speak. The Scriptures tell us to take time regularly to "Be still, and know that I am God" (Ps. 46:10).

We all know how frustrating conversations are when one individual dominates the time. What would you think of someone who called you on the telephone, talked nonstop for ten minutes, then said, "Goodbye," without giving you a chance to get a word in? Too often, our prayers are just like that. We do all the talking and then say "Amen" without giving God a chance to speak. We have the awful habit of telling God what we think and want without waiting to hear what he thinks and wants.

Of course, Christians understand that God has spoken and continues to speak to us through the Scriptures. The authors of Scripture make clear that their writings are God's way of communicating with his people (look carefully, for example, at 1 Jn. 1:1-4 and Heb. 1:1-2). The Bible, after all, is God's *Word.* This means that our primary means of listening to God is reading, studying and meditating on his Word.

Nevertheless, we may also listen to God simply by being still. Having expressed your praise, confessed your sin, communicated your thanks and presented your requests, now say, "Lord, I am listening. Is there anything you would like me to know? Is there something you would like me to do? Talk to me."

God may speak to you in a thought, a flash of insight, some idea or an impulse. He may give you a proneness to move in a particular direction; he may speak in the quieting of anxiety. He might rearrange your whole understanding of a series of events, give you a feeling of his presence, "worthiness," or he may recall to your mind some promise he made in Scripture.

I am a novice at this form of prayer. But God is still able to use what little time I give him. Often, during a period of listening prayer, I will feel a strong impulse to pray for someone, to write a letter or make a visit. Once I had an overwhelming impulse to write a friend of mine who is a doctor. For several days I could not shake this man's name from my thoughts. I prayed for him and I wrote him a letter. A few days later he telephoned to say that his wife had recently died, he was depressed and my letter had arrived at just the right time.

The Lord has so much to say to us. If we will be still, we can know what he is trying to tell us. Why not begin the practice of listening prayer? When you feel the Lord is speaking to you, judge what you feel you should do by Scripture. If it jibes, then go out and earnestly try to perform it.

Practicing the Presence of God A small child knocked on her father's study door. "Yes, daughter, what do you want?" The little girl came into the study and said, "I don't want anything, Dad. I just want to be with you." And with that she promptly curled up at her father's side and went fast to sleep. Now, there is a form of prayer, or perhaps it is better called meditation, that is very like this child's action. We go to God desiring only to be with him, only to see his face. When we pray like that, basking in his magnificent presence, we are ministered to, we gain a deeper sense of our Father-child relationship and we glow from spending time in his presence.

Remember how Moses' face shone when he came down from the mountain after speaking with God? But the longer he stayed away from God the less his face glowed

(2 Cor. 3:7-13). Numbers 6:25 is a related benediction: "The LORD make his face to shine upon you." The apostle Paul, thinking of Moses, urged believers to "be aglow with the Spirit" (Rom. 12:11).

We do not often see this glowing spiritual quality about people. That is because this form of spiritual discipline—simply enjoying the presence of God—is all but a lost art. But it can be regained. You yourself can begin to practice it. You can glow from being in God's presence.

A Communications Revolution Today the world is experiencing a great communications revolution. In recent decades all kinds of instruments have been developed for the sending and receiving of messages. The telegraph, the radio, the telephone, the television, inexpensive paperback books, citizens band radios and satellites have all combined to change the world we live in. They have brought convenience and safety. They have brought people together who are miles apart. But the greatest form of communication, one that promises to bring greater change for the better, one that promises to bring close people who are worlds apart, has yet to be fully discovered and employed. And that is prayer.

It is not recorded that the disciples ever asked Jesus to teach them to heal or preach or work miracles. It was obvious to them that the Lord derived his strength from prayer. If they could learn to pray, all the other things would fall into place. So they said, "Lord, teach us to pray." How about you? Will you ask the Lord to teach you?

4 OUR DAILY PRAYER

No doubt you have heard about the postal service's "Dead Letter Department." That's the place where mail goes when it is not clearly addressed or has insufficient postage and the sender's identity cannot be determined. In the "Dead Letter Department" a letter is opened and its contents examined for clues to the sender's identity. If the return address cannot be determined the letter is destroyed. It never reaches its destination and any requests made by the writer remain unanswered. How about you? Have you ever felt that your prayers end up in a cosmic dead letter department?

Our discussion of prayer has so far discovered the foundations of our confident approach to God in his promises and commands. We have learned from Jesus' teaching and example something of *what* we should pray—praise, confession, thanks, intercession and supplication. We have finally to learn two things about the *manner* of our prayer: we must pray with the mind of Christ and we must not give up.

Jesus said, "Ask, and it will be given you; seek, and you will find; knock, and it will be opened to you. For every one who asks receives, and he who seeks finds, and to him who knocks it will be opened" (Lk. 11:9-10). Here in Jesus' own words we are told how to address our prayers to God so that they will be received and answered.

Ask, and It Will Be Given Throughout the Gospels it is obvious that the Lord was not afraid to ask things of God. He asked for wine at a wedding party. He asked for more bread and fish to feed a crowd. He asked God to heal the blind, the lame, the mute and the possessed. Jesus asked a lot from God. He did not feel that he was imposing. Jesus is telling us to do the same. He is assuring us that we can ask much from God.

I have often been reluctant to ask God for things. I used to think that God was too busy to be troubled over my affairs. I didn't want to bother him. After all, I could not be very important to him. But slowly I have begun to realize that I am a child of God, not an orphan. I am not a disinherited son. I am the child of the King of the universe. And my Father has told me, "Ask, and it will be given you."

Once, while in graduate school, my wife and I were running very short of money. Inflation, a new baby, higher rent, soaring gasoline prices and an electric bill that had more than doubled were taking a big bite out of our income. For several weeks I worried and grew irritable, seeing no way out of our financial plight. But during those weeks I never once prayed about these things. I must have figured seminary students were supposed to be poor. My wife watched quietly as I turned into a tyrant through worry. Finally she simply said, "Steve, why don't we pray about it?" I agreed, and together we told God about it and asked for his help. Things began to happen.

That very afternoon the landlady stopped me while I was emptying the trash. "Steve, for some time now I've been wanting to ask you to be the groundskeeper for this apartment complex. You can do the work between your studies. It'll be good exercise for you. And we'll pay you $2.50 an hour." I accepted and right away we had an extra $25 a week. And I was also getting some much needed exercise.

The next day Kathryn and I found an anonymous letter in our mailbox. In it was a check for over $200. Someone had sent it just to help us out.

Our family was praising the Lord. He had answered our prayers. But then it suddenly dawned on us. The letter was postmarked two days before we had prayed for help and the landlady had been thinking of offering me that job long before we had decided to pray. We began to doubt. Perhaps this new financial help was not an answer to prayer after all. Maybe it was all just a coincidence. Then I remembered a promise of God from Isaiah 65:24: "Before they call I will answer, while they are yet speaking I will hear." What the Lord had done was to go ahead and prepare the answer to our prayers, then he had also prompted our asking. In a sense, the Lord uses our asking to accomplish what he already is eager to do.

Whether it is talent, wisdom, health, money, help or whatever, do not be afraid to ask God for that which you need or feel is important. You won't bother him. He cares about you. You won't impoverish him. The Lord owns the cattle on a thousand hills (Ps. 50:10). "Keep asking," Jesus said, "and it shall be given to you."

Seek, and You Will Find It is true that Christ did a lot of asking in prayer. He asked for bread, wine, healing and a host of other things. But Christ also prayed prayers of *seeking*. In the Garden of Gethsemane the Lord searched for God's will. He said, in effect, "Lord, I ask in prayer that this cup pass from me. Let me not go to the cross, to die. I ask for some other way." But then Jesus began to *seek* in prayer. He said, "Nevertheless not my will, but thine, be done" (Lk. 22:42). Here is an example of Christ searching in prayer. He is looking for God's will. He is trying to find out what the mind of God is so he can obey it.

Jesus told us to pray like this when he said, "If you ask anything in my name, I will do it" (Jn. 14:14). The key to this verse is the phrase, "in my name." Jesus did not say, "Whatever you ask, I will do it." He said, "If you ask anything *in my name,* I will do it." The Greek word used here for "in my name" means more than just a label. If you called on someone's name in the Greek world you were calling on their actual presence. So Jesus was saying, "If you ask anything in my presence, I will do it."

As Christians, we believe in the presence of Christ. We believe Jesus is with us by the power of the Holy Spirit. Through this power, being aware of the presence of Christ, we are to take on Jesus' attitude in our requests. Philippians 2:5 tells us to "have this mind among yourselves, which is yours in Christ Jesus, who, though he was in the form of God, did not count equality with God a thing to be grasped, but emptied himself, taking the form of a servant."

Here is the secret of prayer. When we pray we should ask with the attitude of Christ. Jesus said, "If you ask anything in my name [or in my presence, or rather, in my mind,] I will do it." Thus prayer is not overcoming God's reluctance. It is taking hold of his eagerness. It is not presenting your arguments in order to make God change his mind. Prayer is searching for the mind of Christ and then asking in accordance with it.

When confronted with a need, it is not a good idea to go right out and pray about it by telling God what you want. You may not know the mind of Christ in the matter. You may ask in the flesh and not in the Spirit. So first ask the Lord to reveal to you his mind. Say, "Lord, here is a need. Teach me your mind. Show me how to pray about this." Sometimes I spend days just seeking how to pray about something. Then when I've found the mind of Christ, the asking prayer may be brief and to the point.

Imagine that you are in a rowboat fifteen feet from the

shore. You throw an anchor ashore and pull yourself to the dock. Who moved? You or the shore? You did. Seeking prayer works like this as well. You throw out an anchor to God. You seek in prayer, in Scripture, in fellowship, in obedience and you pull yourself to God's mind and ask in it.

The apostle Paul knew how to seek in prayer. He may have said, "God, I am sick. I have this thorn in my flesh." Three times Paul went to God and asked to be healed. And there in God's presence Paul began to know the mind of Christ. The situation was not changed for Paul. Paul was changed within the situation. He quit asking to be healed. He started asking for the strength to bear the affliction for the glory of God (2 Cor. 12:7-9).

In your own prayer life you too will want to learn seeking prayer. You will want to learn to pray in Christ's name, in his presence and mind. When you are facing a need, take your problem directly to God. Do not limit him by telling him what to do about it. Just envision the problem in both your hands. Then envision God. Think of his presence. Meditate on his marvelous love and power. Then lift up the problem into God's presence and leave it there.

When an author submits a manuscript to a publisher, the publisher first edits it. The editors may shorten it by deleting material, correct the spelling and verify facts. Finally, when the manuscript is in its best form, the book will be printed. God has editing rights over our prayers as well. He will receive them like a teacher does a term paper. He will edit them, correct them, bring them in line with his will and then hand them back to us to be resubmitted in asking prayer. And when we relinquish our will to God's and pray seeking like this, Jesus assures us that we shall find.

Knock, and It Shall Be Opened Knocking, persistent knocking, is sometimes necessary to open doors through prayer. There is more involved in answering prayer than your will and God's will. There are other forces like hard hearts and uncooperative wills. You might be praying that God will save your son. But your son's heart is stony toward God. You want him saved. And there is nothing God would like better than to save him, but there is a barrier. God has given your son a free will. He will not violate it by forcing himself on anyone. And for the time being your son's cold heart has chosen to leave God out.

There is also the barrier of the satanic. The Bible says, "We are not contending against flesh and blood, but against the principalities, against the powers, against the world rulers of this present darkness, against the spiritual hosts of wickedness in the heavenly places" (Eph. 6:12). An example of how satanic forces can hinder answers to prayer is found in Daniel 10. There the prophet prayed for more than twenty days without any answer. Finally, an angel visited him and explained the reason for the delay. He said, "O Daniel, man greatly beloved, . . . from the first day that you set your mind to understand and humbled yourself before your God, your words have been heard, and I have come because of your words. The prince of the kingdom of Persia withstood me twenty-one days; but Michael, one of the chief princes, came to help me . . . so I . . . came" (Dan. 10:11-13). Satanic powers hindered an answer to prayer. And here we must come to Scripture with a sense of wonder. There is much about this world and about spiritual warfare that we do not understand. But God has revealed that satanic forces can hinder prayer and can be defeated only through prolonged and earnest prayer (see Mt. 17:21 and Mk. 9:28-29).

The book of Job is perhaps the best place in Scripture to study knocking prayer. Righteous Job loses his children, his friends, property and health. Satan has horribly afflicted him. Although his wife urges him to curse God and die, Job blesses God. And throughout the drama he prays a knocking prayer. "Oh, that I knew where I might find him, that I might come even to his seat! I would lay my case before him and fill my mouth with arguments. I would learn what he would answer me" (Job 23:3-5).

Thus Job begins to *knock* in prayer. He blindly gropes for God. He patiently and sometimes impatiently cries out for deliverance. Again and again Job reaches for God in prayer. Though his body is wasting away, though all seems lost, though he cannot understand, Job has faith in God. His heart is filled with hope and he says, "I know that my Redeemer lives, and at last he will stand upon the earth; and after my skin has been thus destroyed, then from my flesh I shall see God" (Job 19:25-26).

Thus with hope, faith and persistence Job continues to knock in prayer. The most grievous pain for Job is the lost fellowship with God, his friend. Finally God comes and reveals himself to Job. Though the Lord does not explain the affliction, he does heal Job and restores and increases his fortune. Job's persistent prayer was not in vain. This illustrates what Jesus later promised: it will be opened to those that knock.

Perhaps Jesus was thinking of Job when he told this parable:

> *Which of you who has a friend will go to him at midnight and say to him, "Friend, lend me three loaves; for a friend of mine has arrived on a journey, and I have nothing to set before him"; and he will answer from within, "Do not bother me; the door is now shut, and my children are with me in bed; I cannot get up and give you anything"? I tell you, though he will not get up and give him anything because he is his friend, yet because of his importunity he will rise and give him whatever he needs. (Lk. 11:5-8)*

Here Jesus teaches us the value of persistent prayer. When confronted with closed doors, hard hearts, and satanic barriers it becomes imperative to *knock* in prayer.

The New American Standard Bible rightly translates (in a marginal note) Luke 11:9[3] as "Keep knocking." This implies a repeated action, not a one-time effort. And so our knocking prayers must be persistently repeated.

Why must we pray persistently? Do we do so to coerce God into helping us? In order to persuade him to change his mind? No! Persistent prayer is better understood as unleashing spiritual power. Have you ever tried to open a rusty water valve? It is frozen stiff with corrosion. You strain and strain at it but little progress is made. So you rest awhile, then try again. With all your might you grip the handle and twist. It budges a bit. You rest again, then return for another try. Slight progress is made and a trickle of water begins to flow. After yet another rest you have a try at it again. More progress. And so you persist until the valve is wide open and the water is on full. Prayer works like this as well. To persist in prayer is to open more and more the spiritual channels through which the power of God can flow. Closed doors, hard hearts and satanic obstacles give way to the relentless pressure applied by God and the kneeling Christian.

The Bible gives us numerous accounts of knocking prayer. Moses, during a battle, lifted up his hands and prayed continuously until victory was won (Ex. 17:8-16). Daniel engaged in earnest supplication twenty-one days (Dan. 10). And in Acts we are told that the church prayed all evening for Peter's release from prison (Acts 12). Even now many people are praying, knocking on God's door for many things. Some of them have been praying for months and years. Missionary societies have been praying for years that China will reopen for the church. Saints are praying persistently for a real revival to wake up the Western church. Mothers are praying for erring children and husbands are knocking on heaven's door on behalf of their wives. In each case, things appear all but hopeless. Hearts seem too cold. Barriers seem too large. But the power will begin to trickle. Who knows but that just one more twist will open things up all the way?

Day by Day In the rock opera *Godspell* there is a song called "Day by Day" that expresses well what our attitude and practice in prayer should be.

Day by Day, day by day
Oh, dear Lord, three things I pray
To see Thee more clearly
Love Thee more dearly
Follow Thee more nearly
Day by Day.[6]

The music is new but few realize that the prayer has been around for over seven hundred years. Richard of Chichester in the thirteenth century prayed, "O most merciful Friend, Brother, and Redeemer, may I know Thee more clearly, love Thee more dearly, and follow Thee more nearly." "Day by Day" is just an old prayer put to new music. The world needs more Christians who will seek, ask and knock. Jesus did not say we should sit around and wait for things to fall into our mouths like a ripe grape. He said seek, ask, knock. And when you seek and keep on seeking, you find. When you ask and keep on asking, you receive. And when you knock and keep on knocking, the door is opened.

Thus all our praying needs to be a day-by-day experience. It needs to be an asking experience in which we see God more clearly, a seeking experience in which we love him more dearly and a knocking experience in which we follow him more nearly.

What Prayer Is Prayer is silent or spoken praise directed to God. It is the penitent confession of the guilty. It is also thanksgiving. It is personal supplication, intercession, constant heavenward groaning.

Prayer is the listening ear and the silent revel of the soul in the presence of God. It is seeking. It is also asking and knocking. Prayer is all this and more, so much more. It is often eloquent and loud, insistent and public. But it is also mute and sometimes closeted. Most of all, prayer is the dialog between a person and the Savior who loves him.

You are invited to seek the Lord in prayer. If you do, you will make the delightful discovery that God is seeking you. Love the Lord and you will find that he loves you. Call on his name and you will find that he has been calling you. There is nothing to hinder your getting acquainted with God but your will.

NOTES

[1]Ernest Hemingway, "A Clean, Well-lighted Place" in *The Snows of Kilimanjaro and Other Stories* (New York: Scribner, 1964), pp. 29-33.
[2]C. S. Lewis, *Letters to Malcolm: Chiefly on Prayer* (London: Collins, Fontana, 1963), p. 18.
[3]Sam Walter Foss, "The Prayer of Cyrus Brown" in *Stars to Steer By,* ed. Louis Untermeyer (New York: Harcourt, Brace & Co., 1941), pp. 301-02.
[4]Voltaire, *Candide and Other Writings,* ed. Haskell M. Block (New York: Random, Modern Lib., 1956), p. 149.
[5]John Paterson, *How to Pray Together* (Downers Grove, Ill.: Inter-Varsity Pr., 1951), pp. 5-6.
[6]"Day by Day" from *Godspell* (New York: Bell Records, n.d.).

SUGGESTED READING

The following books represent a variety of perspectives on prayer and related topics.

Allen, Charles L. *All Things Are Possible through Prayer*. Old Tappan, N.J.: Revell, Spire, 1958.

Carothers, Merlin. *Power in Praise*. Plainfield, N.J.: Logos, 1972.

Christenson, Evelyn and Blake, Viola. *What Happens When Women Pray*. Wheaton, Ill.: Victor, 1975.

Hallesby, O. *Prayer*. Minneapolis: Augsburg, 1931.

Lawrence, Brother. *The Practice of the Presence of God*. Old Tappan, N.J.: Revell, Spire, 1958.

Lewis, C. S. *Letters to Malcolm: Chiefly on Prayer*. London: Collins, Fontana, 1963.

Murray, Andrew. *With Christ in the School of Prayer*. Old Tappan, N.J.: Revell, Spire, 1953.

Paterson, John. *How to Pray Together*. Downers Grove, Ill.: InterVarsity Pr., 1951.

Prater, Arnold. *You Can Pray As You Ought.* New York: Nelson, 1977.

Rinker, Rosalind. *Conversational Prayer.* Waco, Tex.: Word Bks., 1970.

____________. *Prayer: Conversing with God.* Grand Rapids, Mich.: Zondervan, 1970.

Torrey, Reuben A. *How to Pray.* Old Tappan, N.J.: Revell, Spire, 1900.

____________. *The Tower of Prayer.* Grand Rapids, Mich.: Zondervan, 1971.

Wallis, Arthur. *God's Chosen Fast.* Fort Washington, Penn.: Chr. Lit., 1968.

White, John. *Daring to Draw Near.* Downers Grove, Ill.: InterVarsity Pr., 1977.